I0509457

This book belongs to:

. . . .

Have Fun And Relax

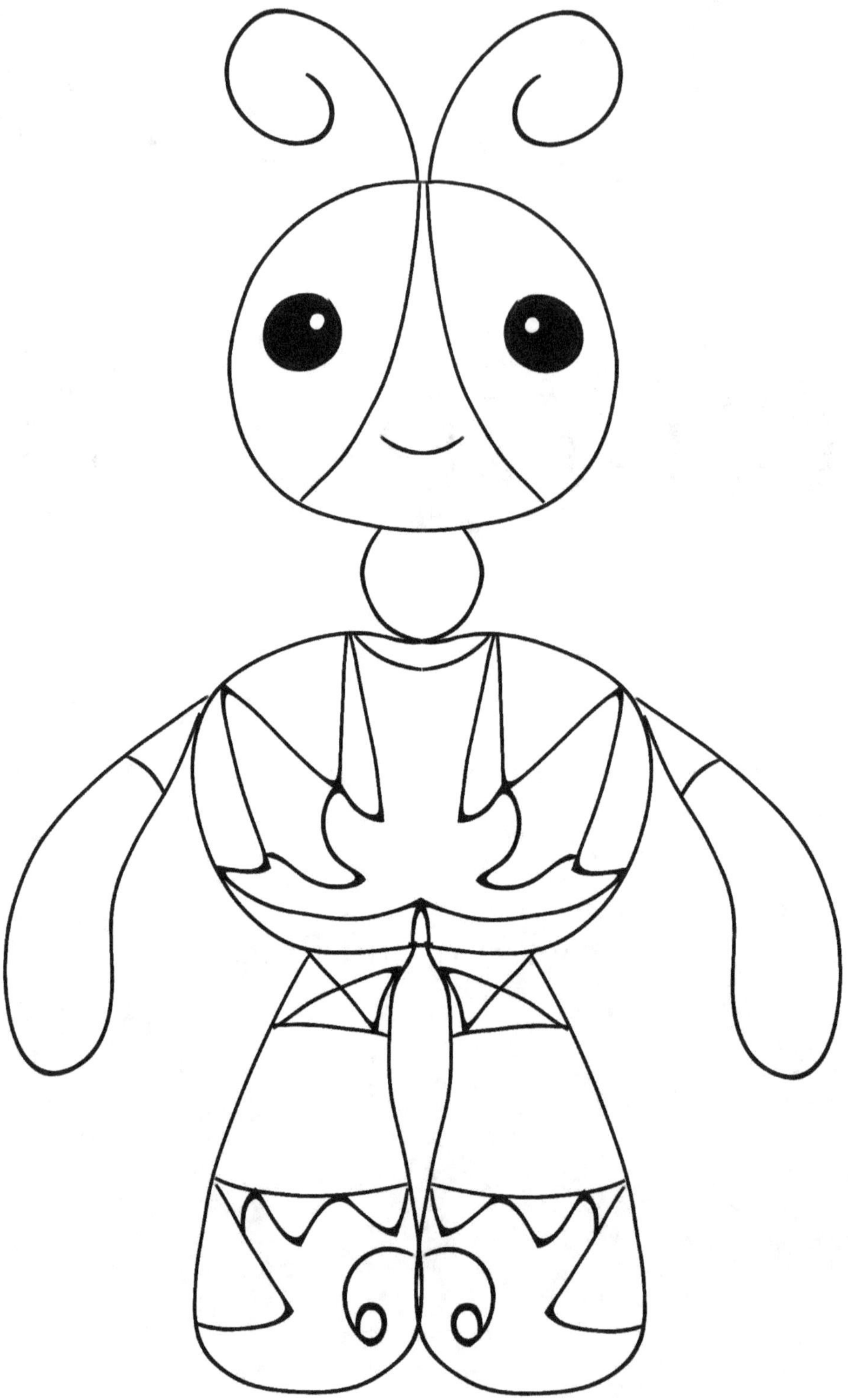

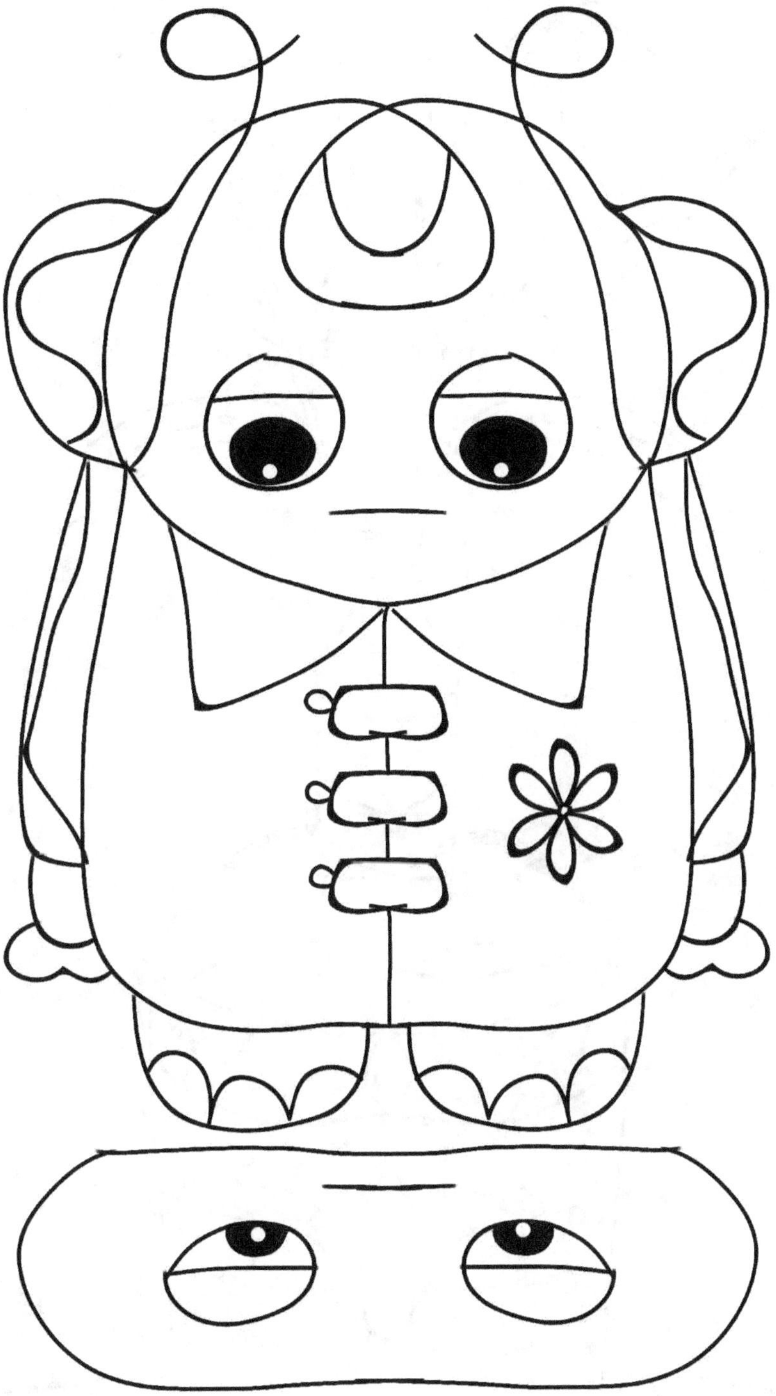

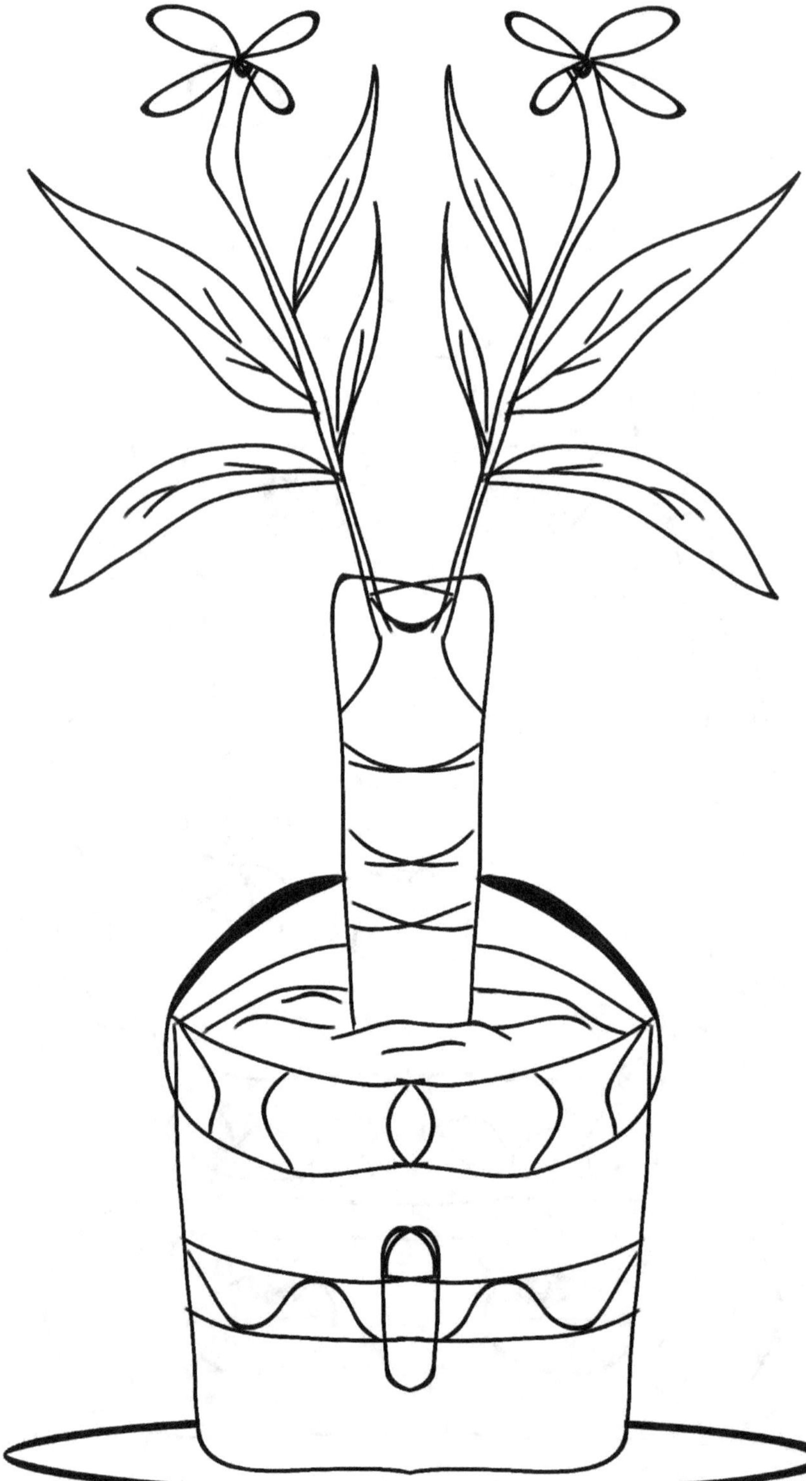

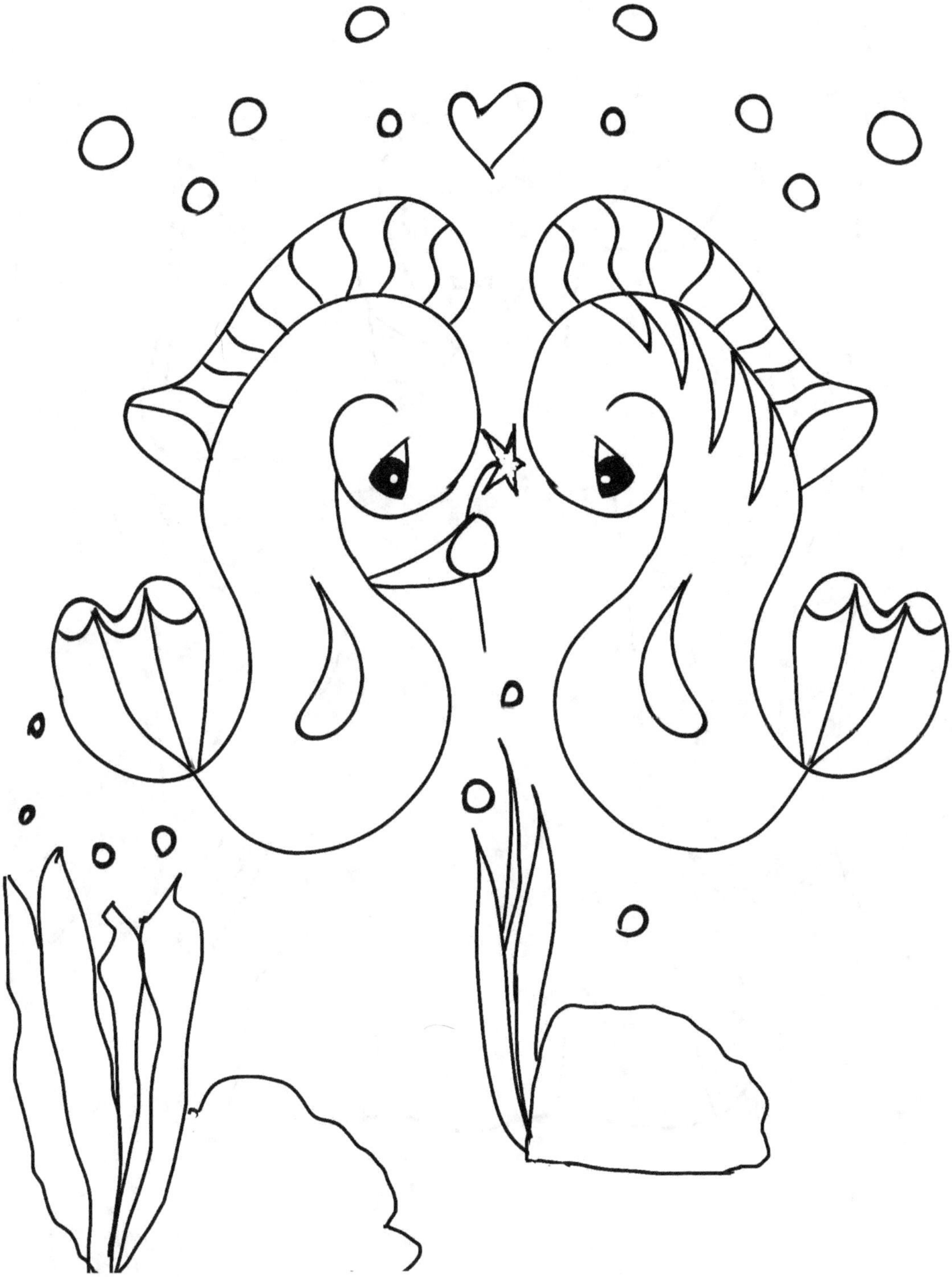

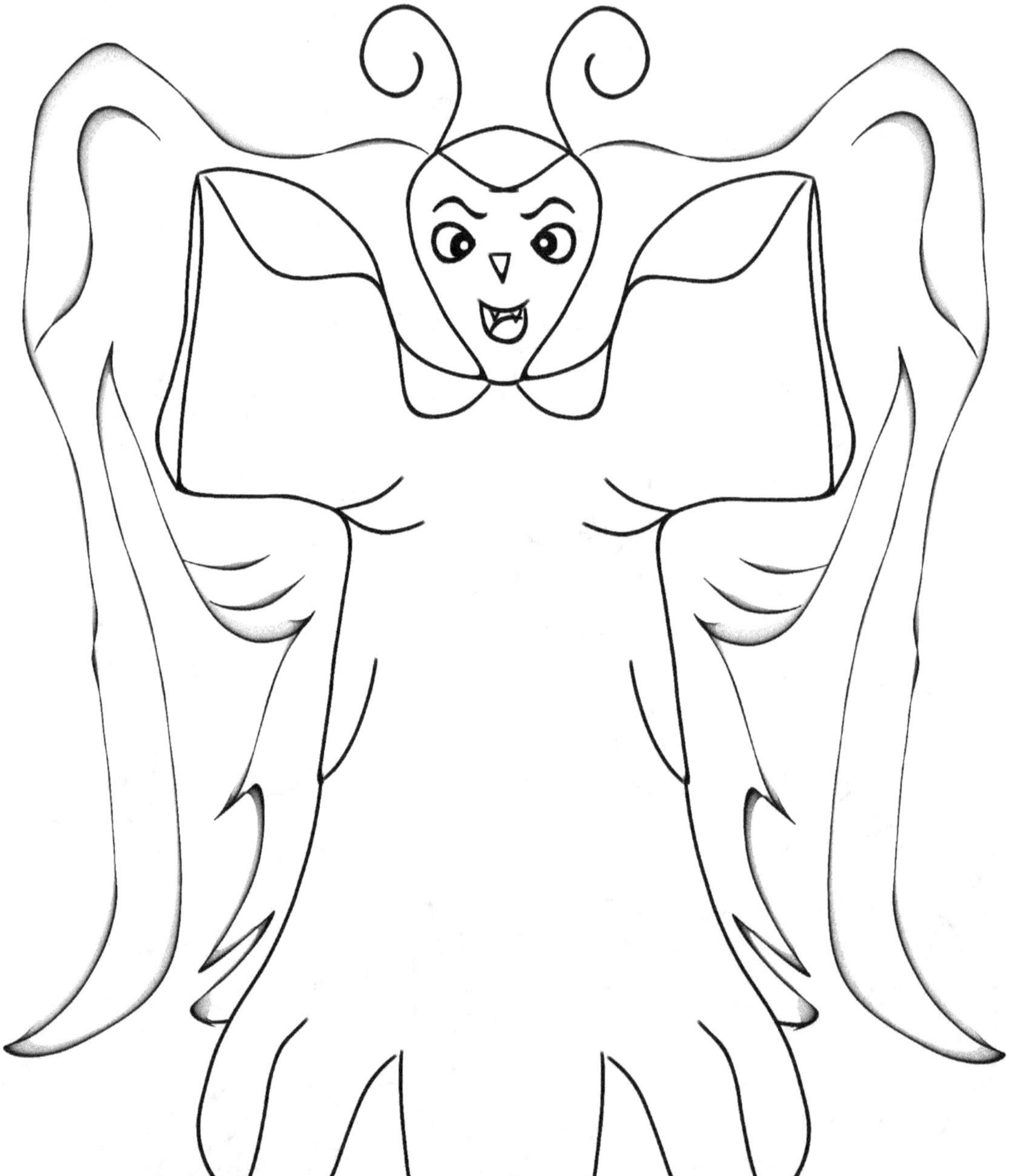

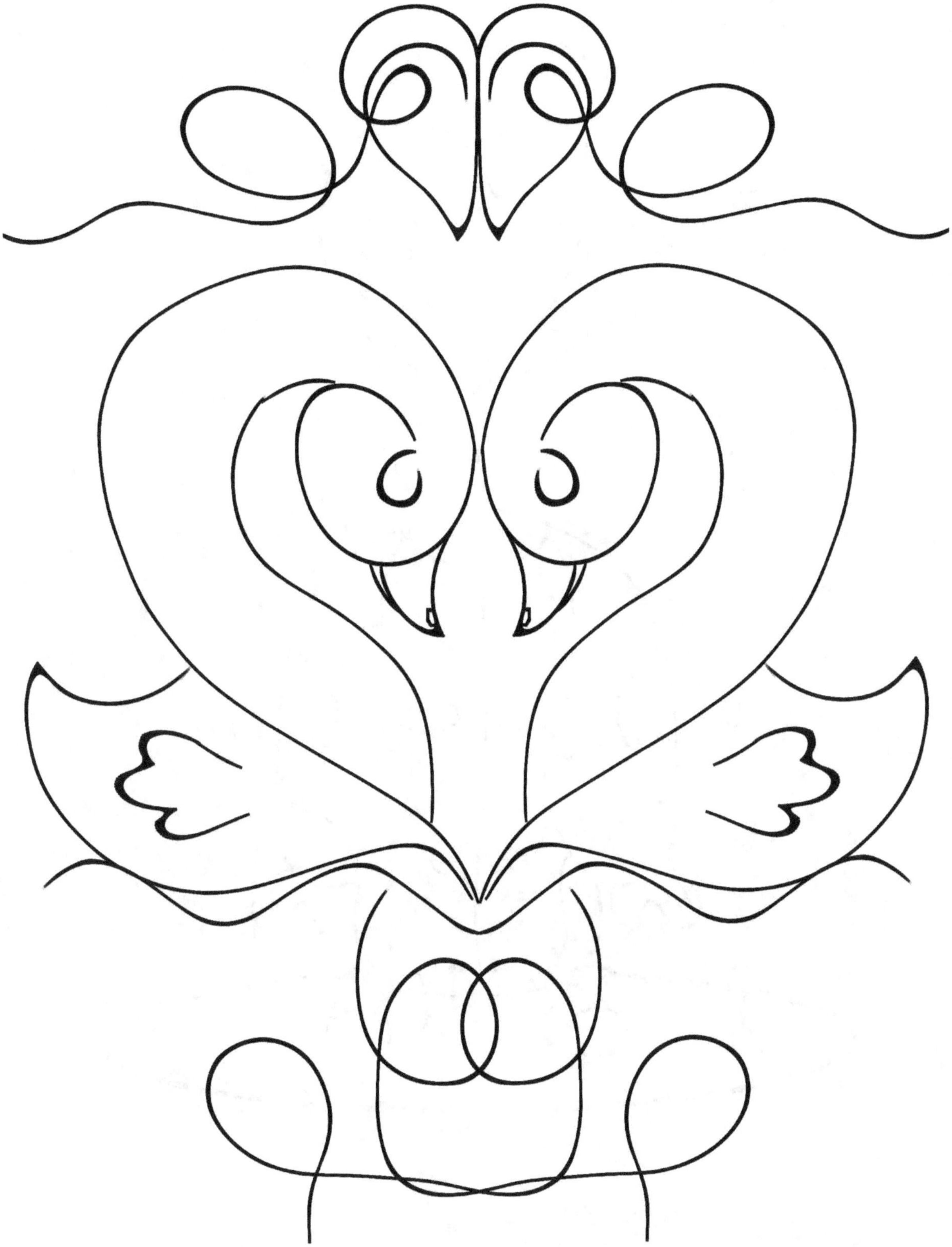

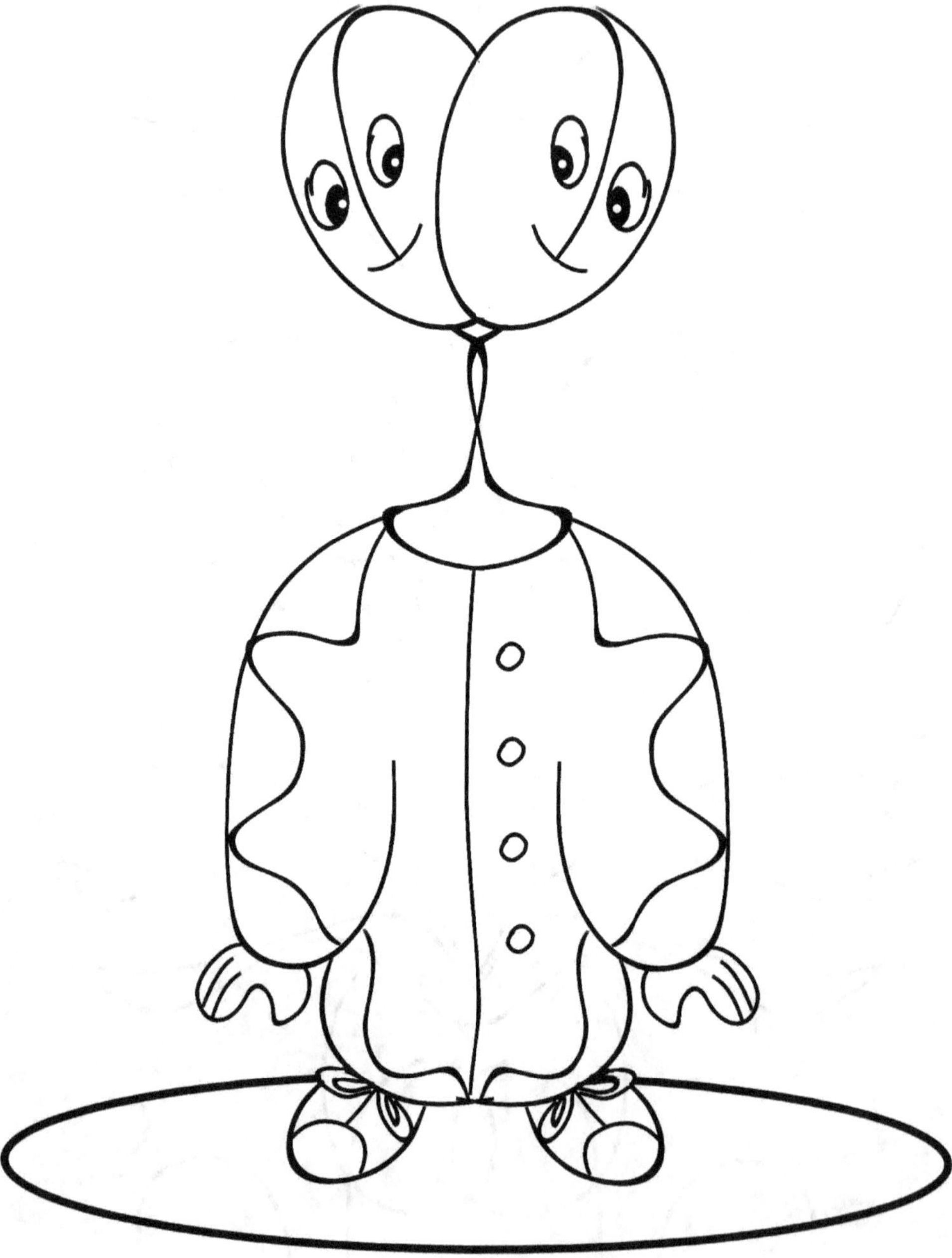

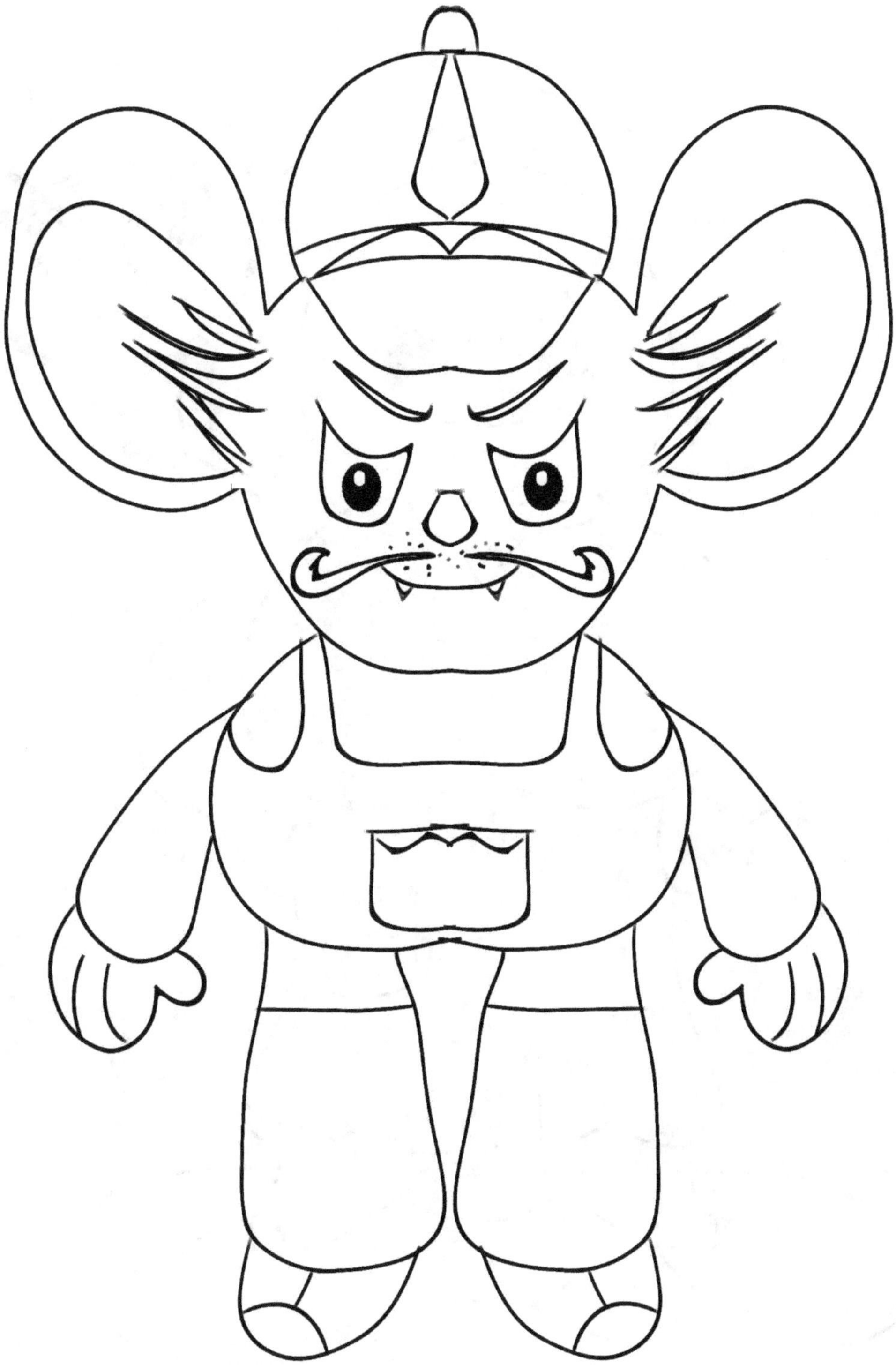

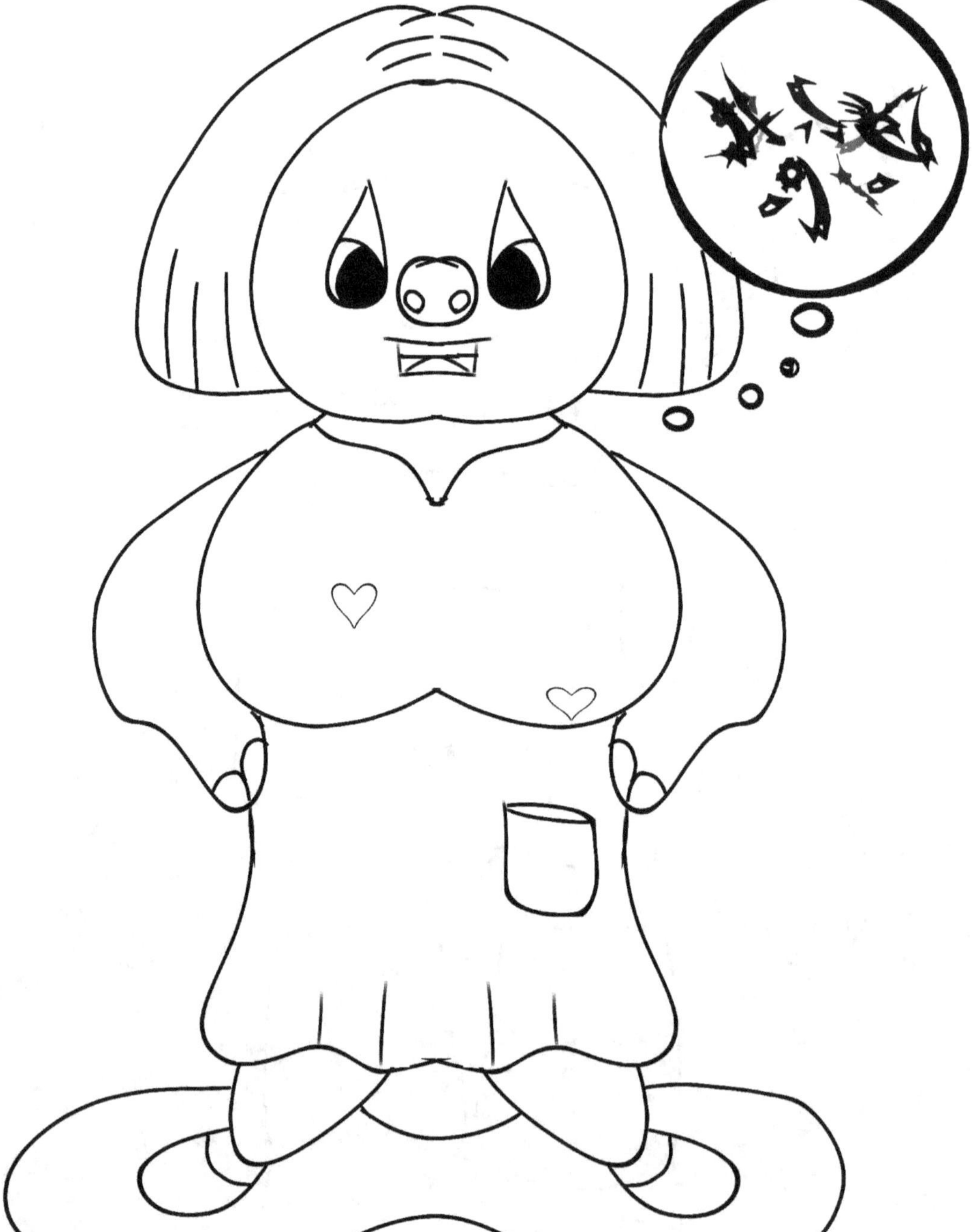

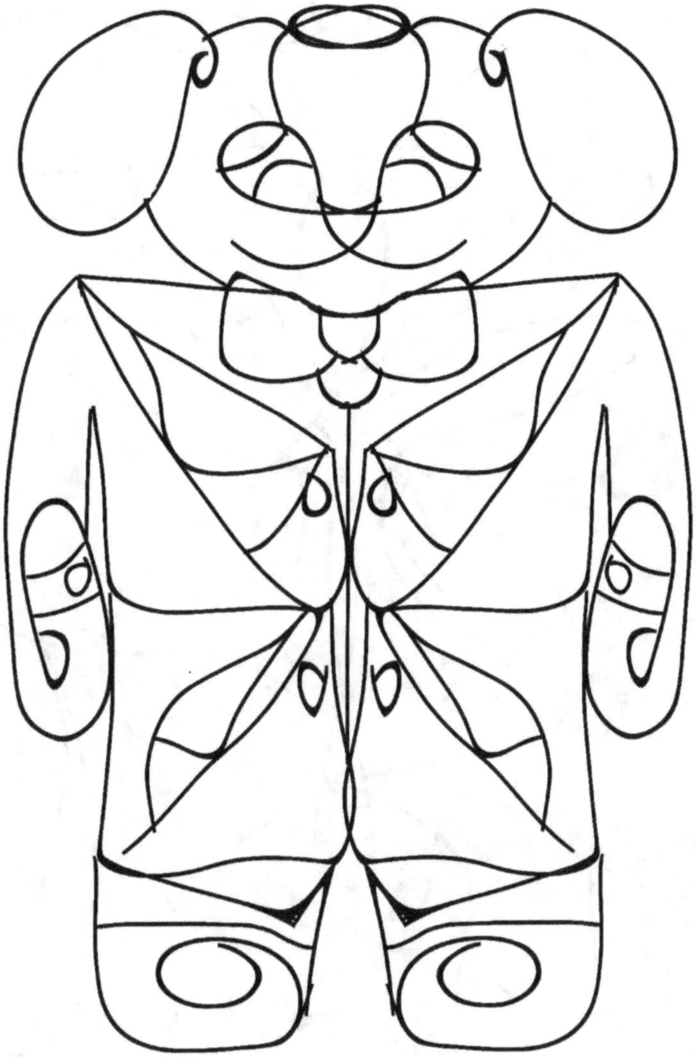

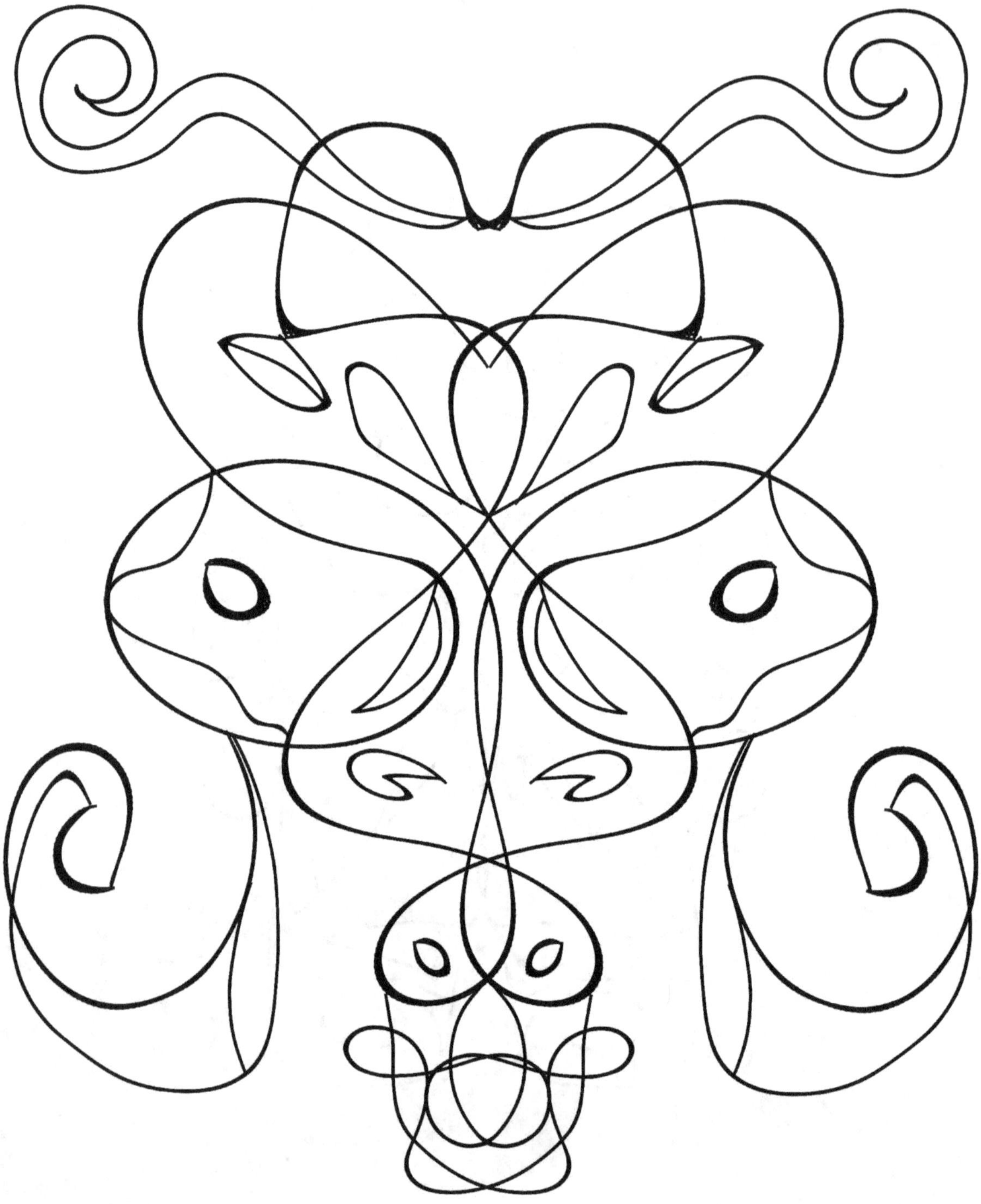

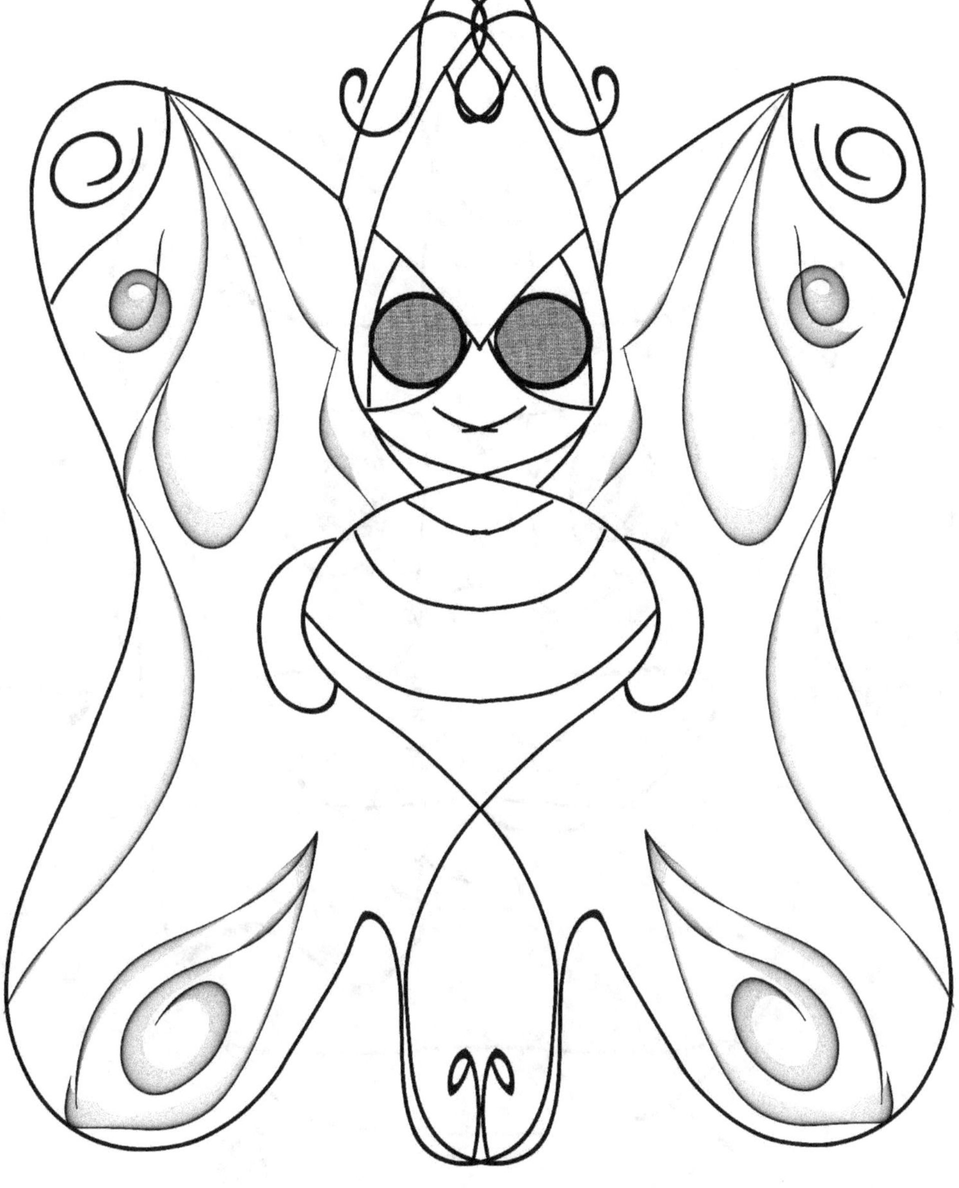

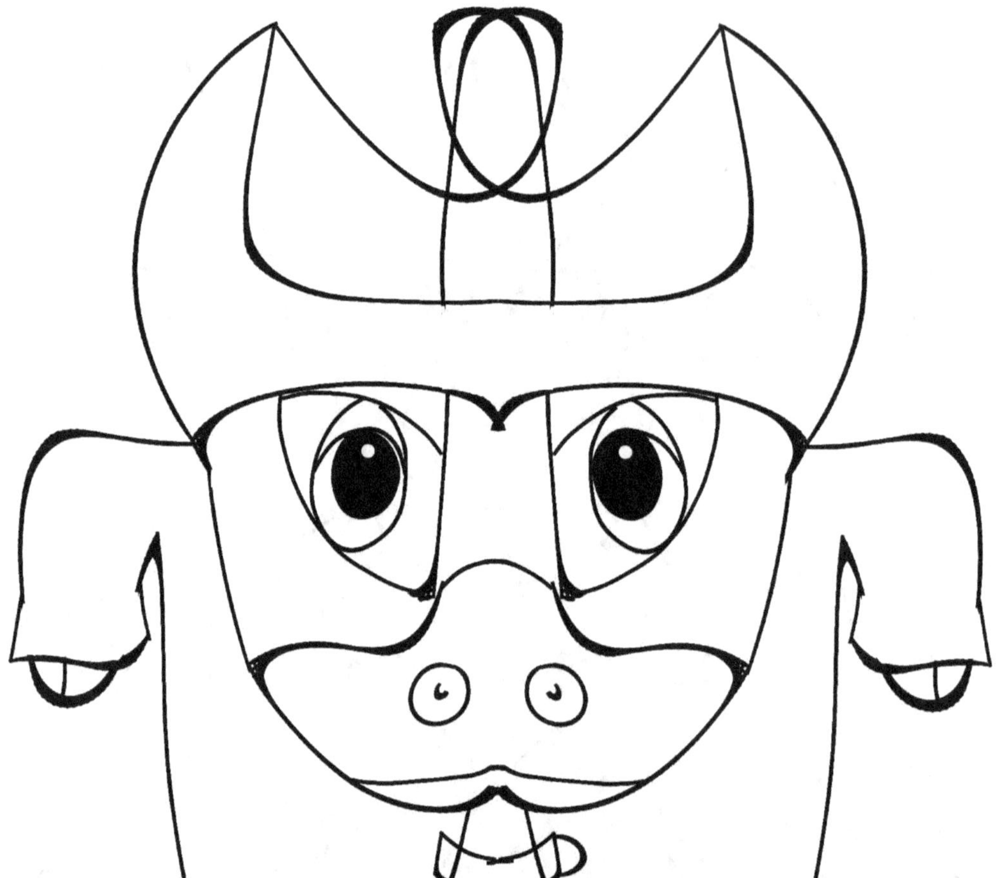

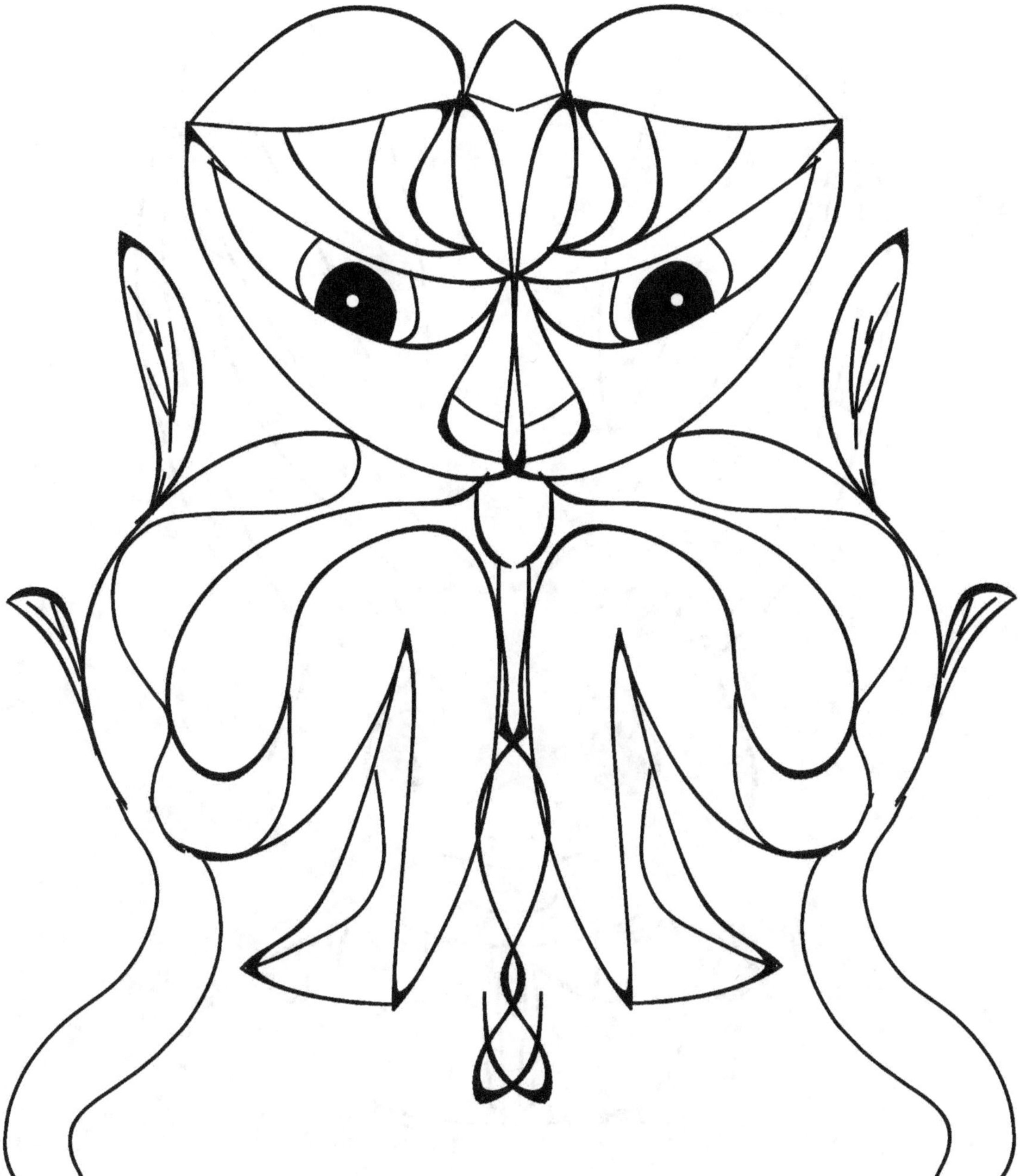

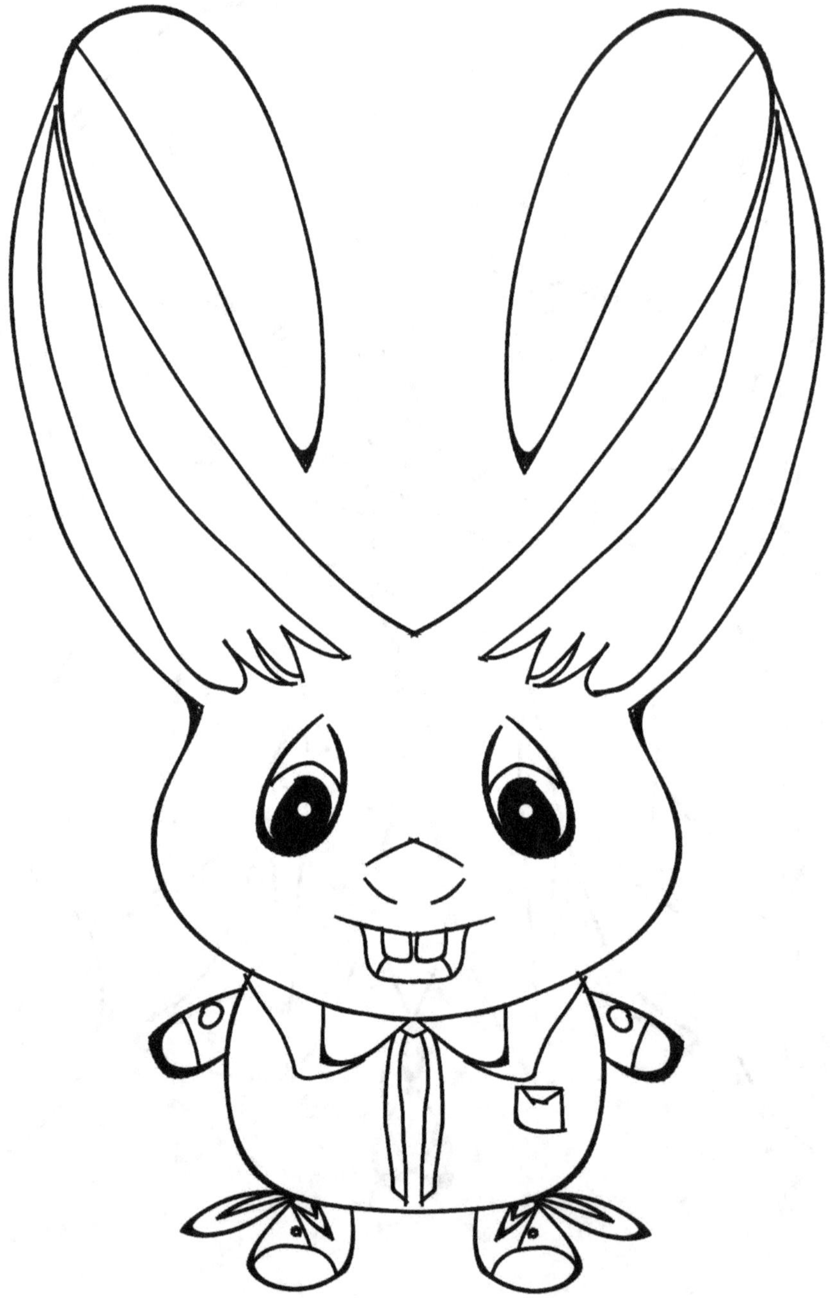

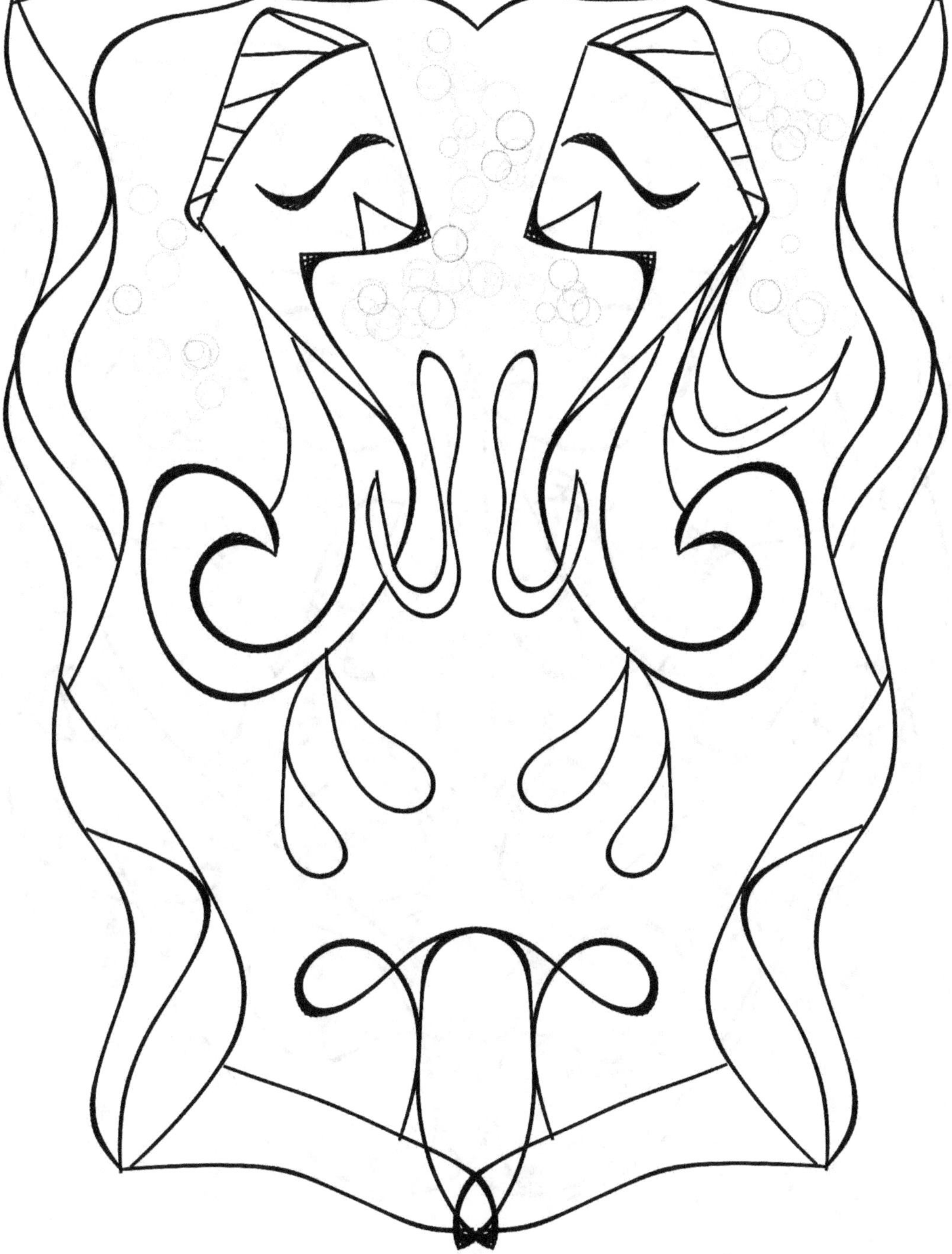

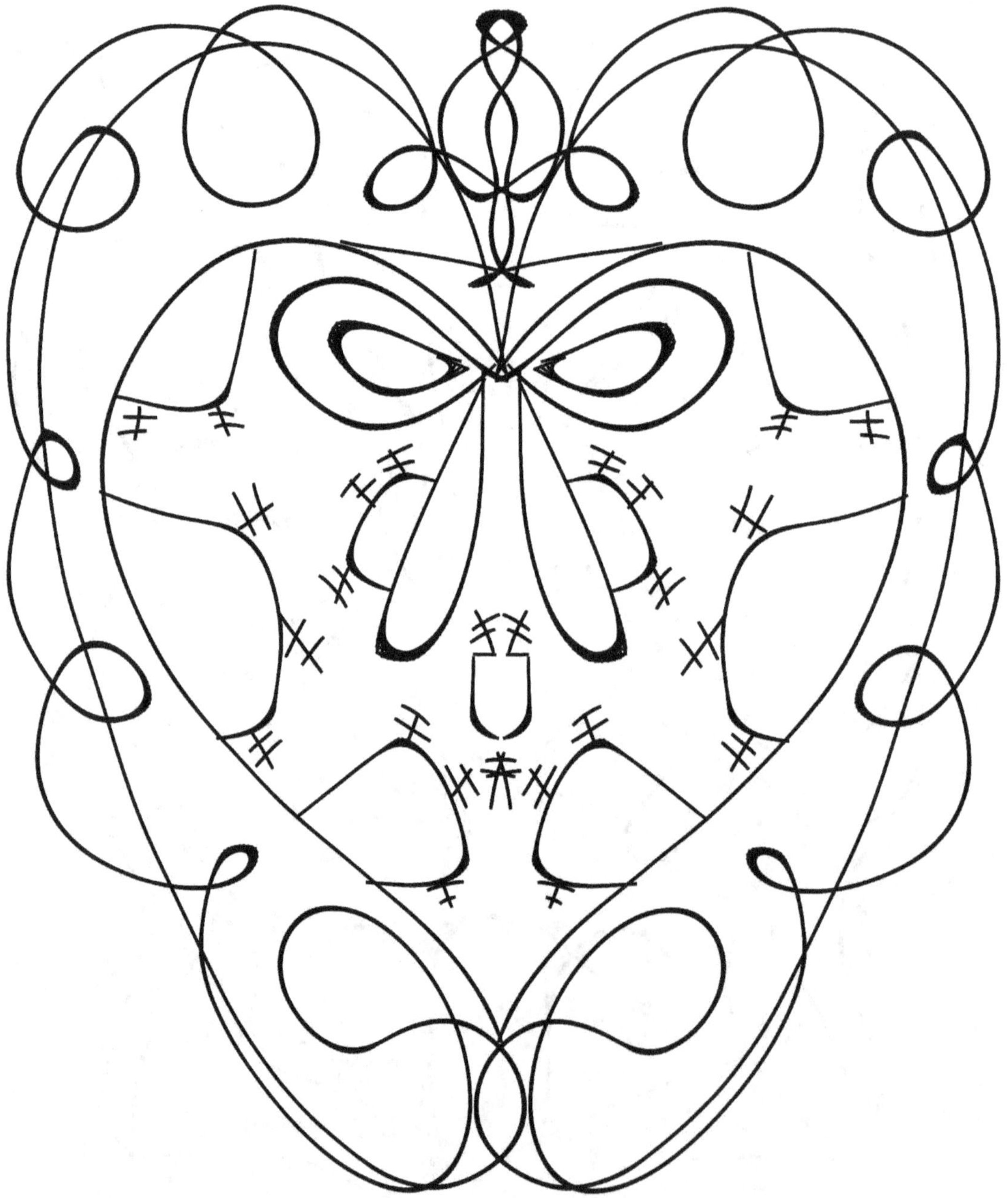

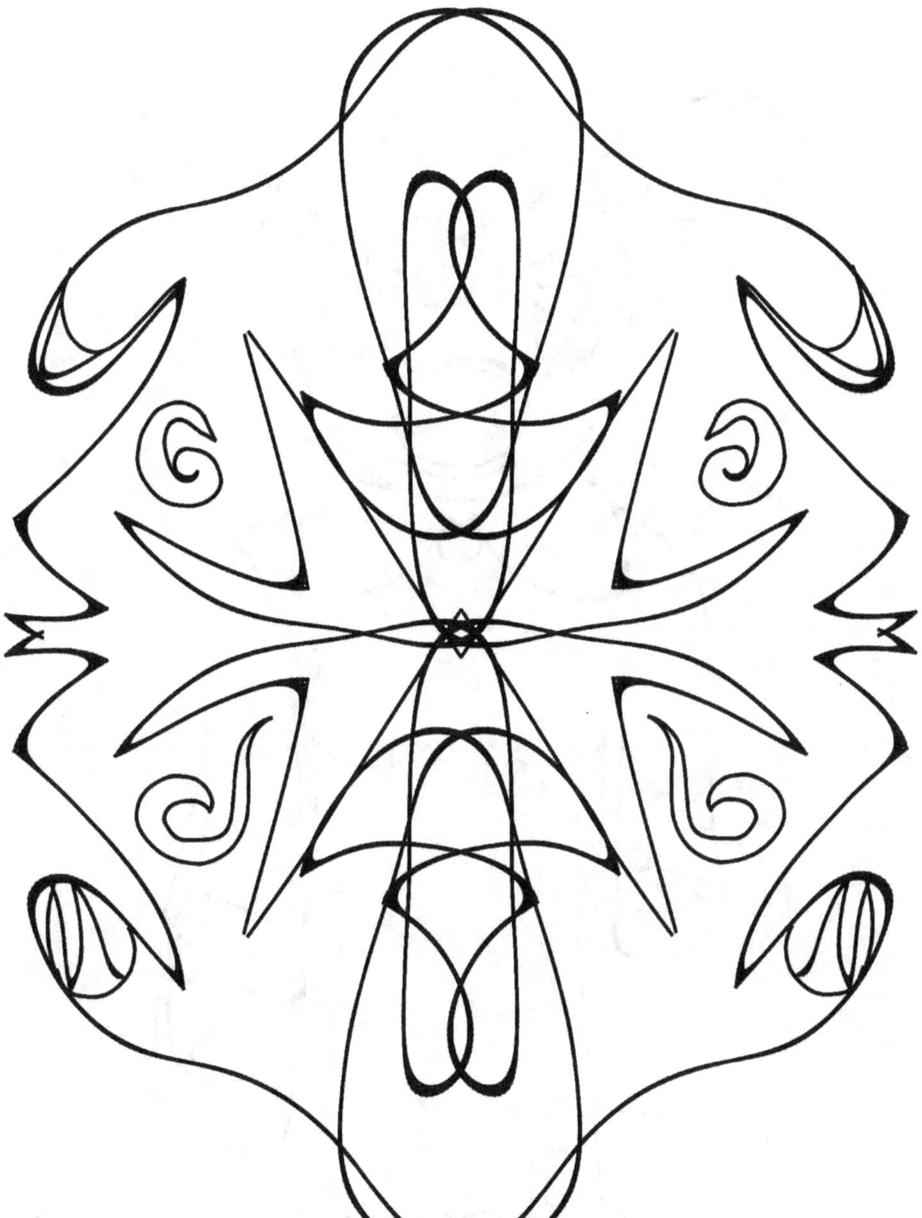

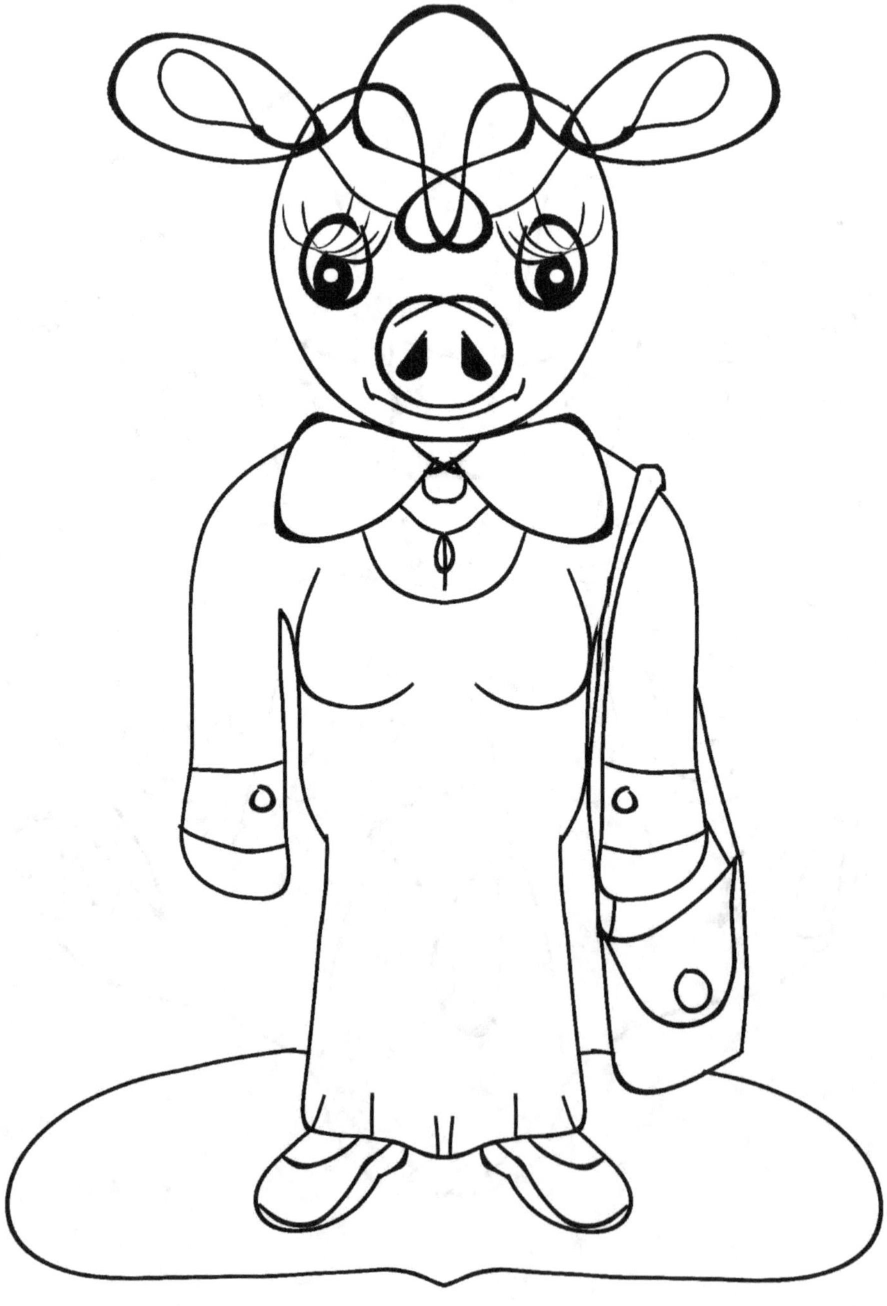

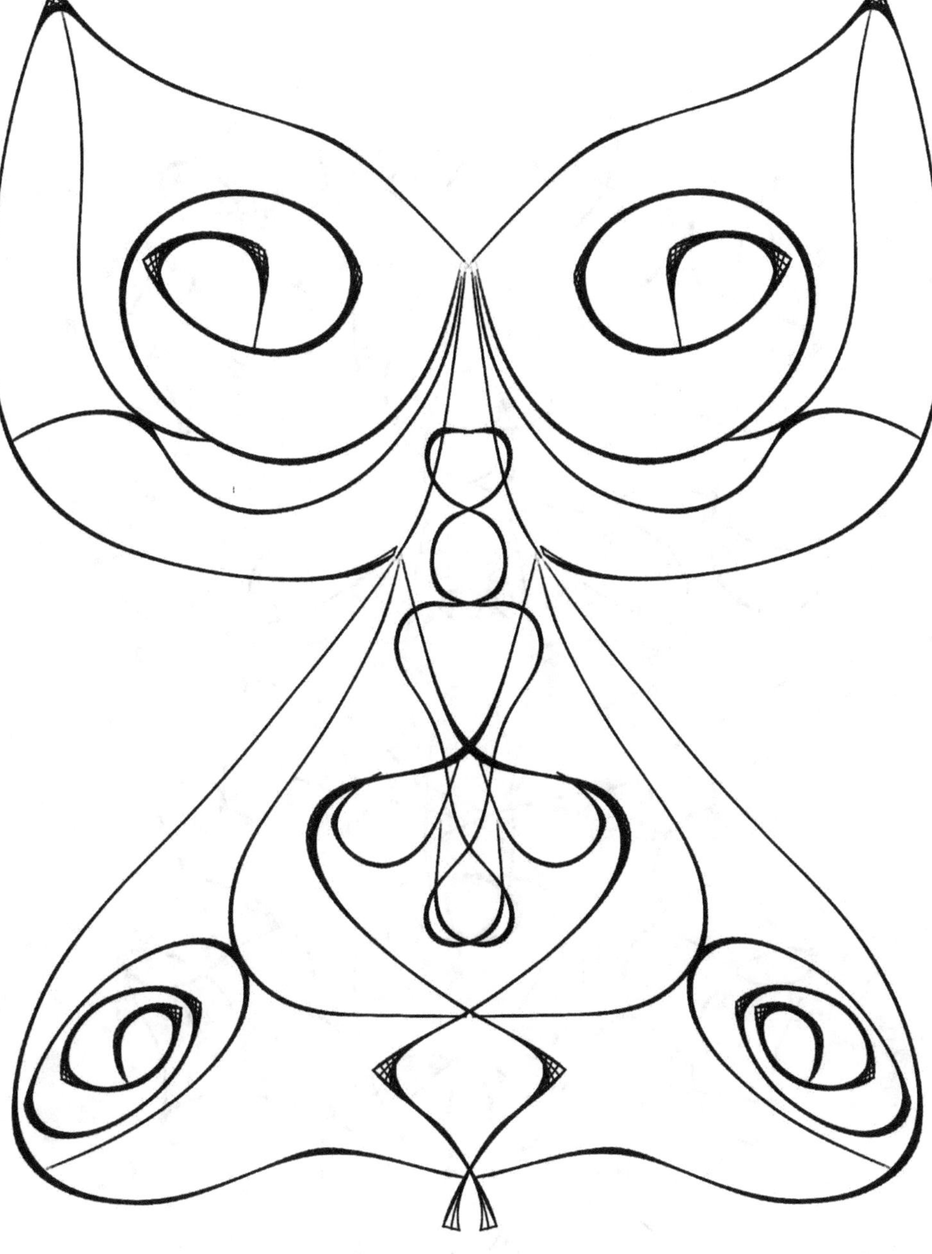

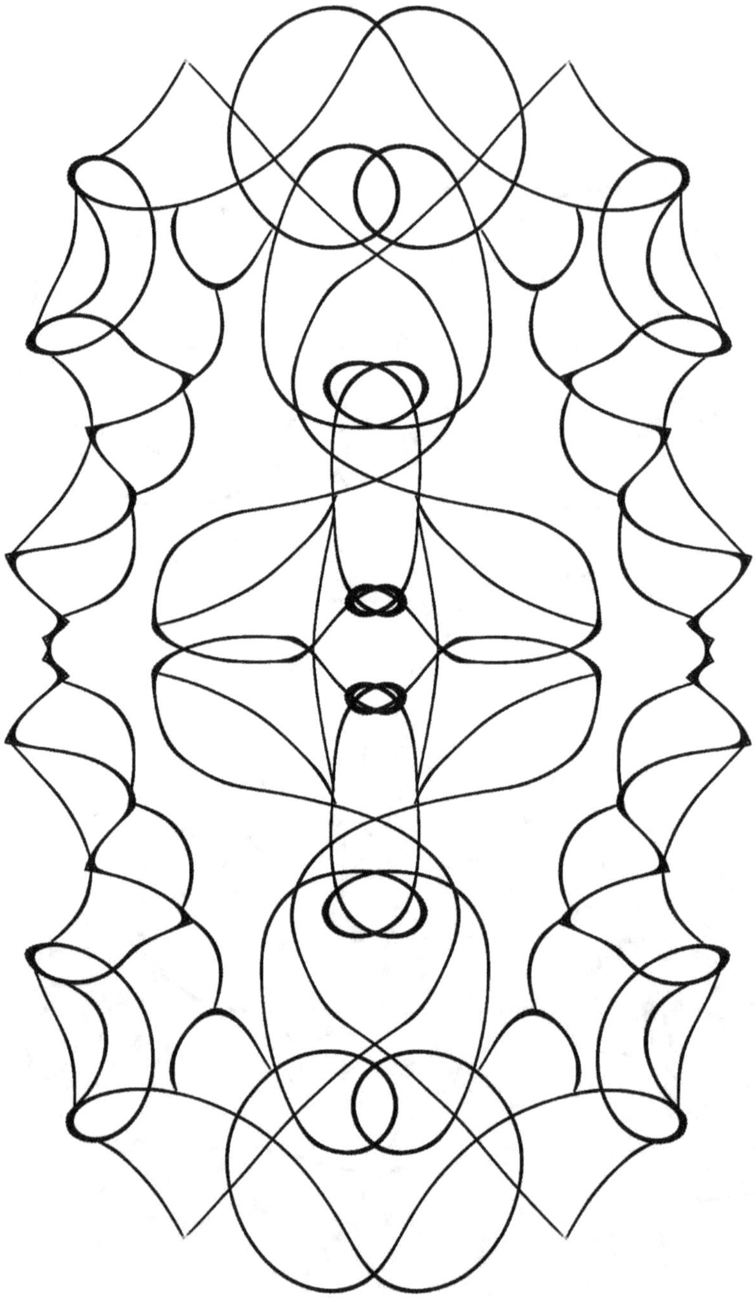

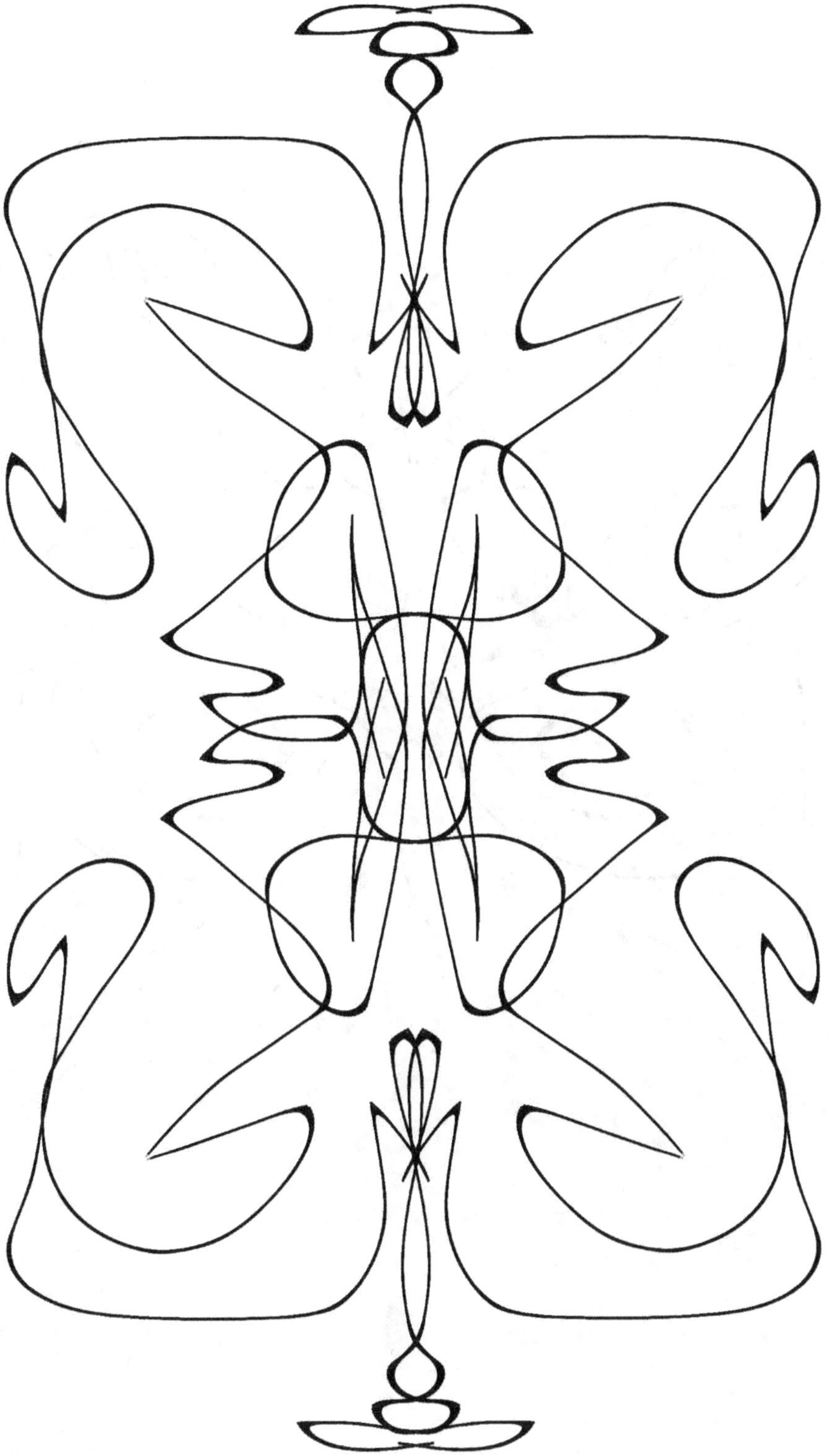

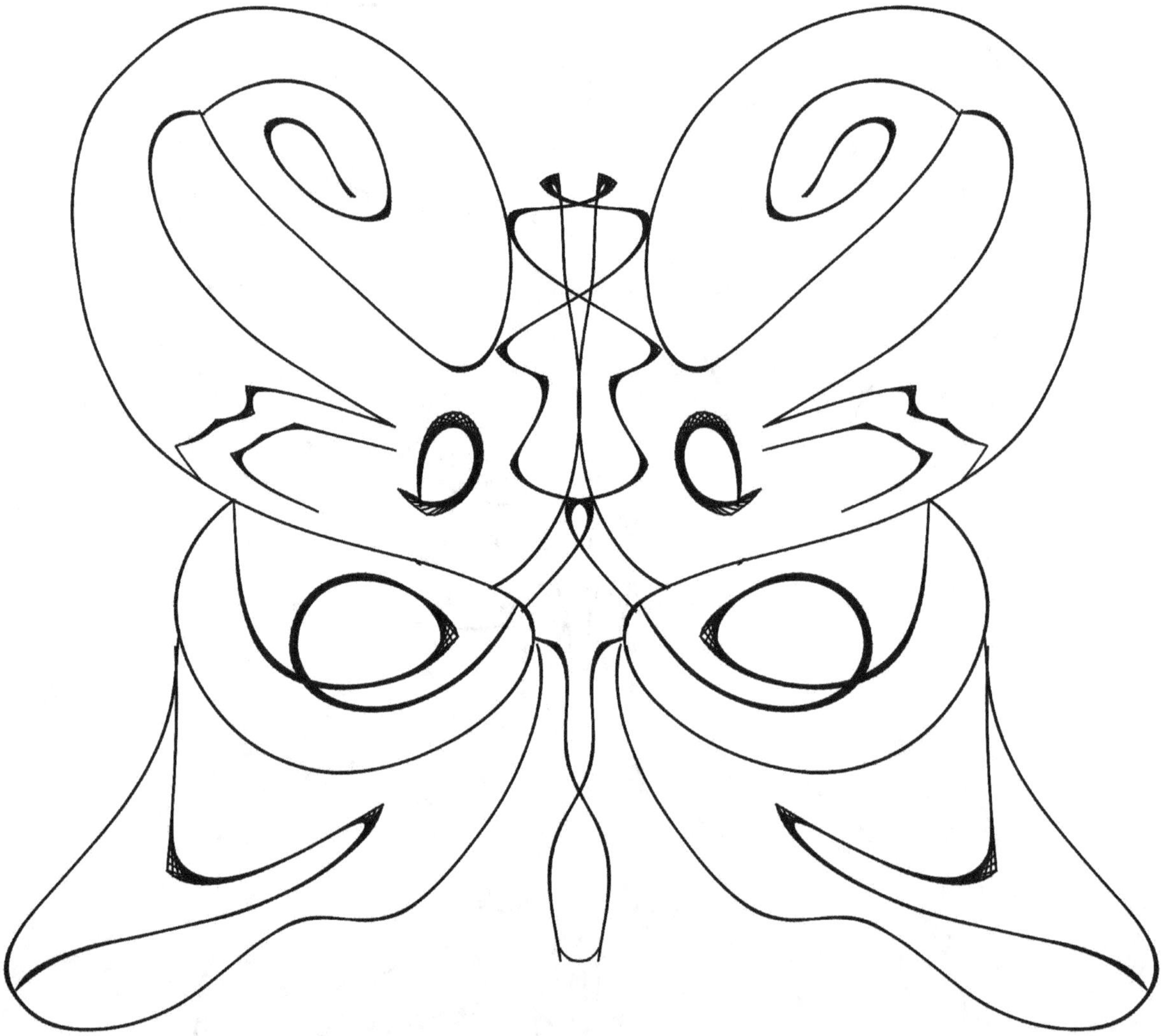

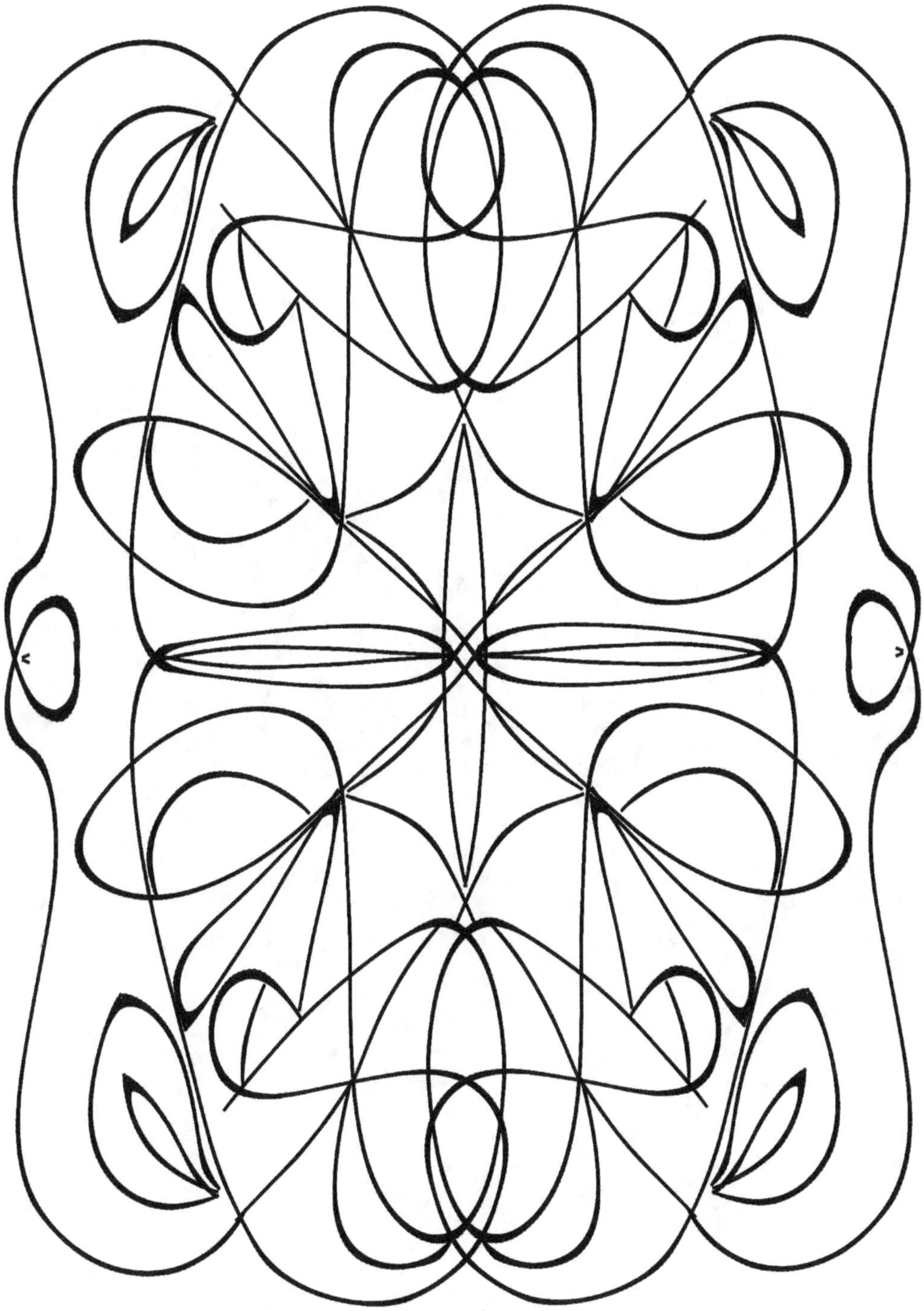

www.ingramcontent.com/pod-product-compliance
Lightning Source LLC
Chambersburg PA
CBHW081710220526
45466CB00009B/2944
* 9 7 8 1 6 6 1 7 4 5 5 9 2 *